Author:

Fiona Macdonald studied history at Cambridge University and at the University of East Anglia, England. She has taught in schools and colleges and has written numerous books for children.

Illustrator:

Mark Bergin was born in Hastings in 1961. He studied at Eastbourne College of Art, England and has specialized in historical reconstruction since leaving art school in 1983. He lives in East Sussex with his wife and family.

Series creator:

David Salariya is an illustrator, designer, and author. He is the founder of the Salariya Book Company, which specializes in the creation and publication of books for young people, from babies to teenagers, under its imprints Book House, Scribblers and Scribo.

Editor: **Penny Clarke**

Published by **S** SCRIBO
25 Marlborough Place, Brighton BN1 1UB
A division of Book House, an imprint of
The Salariya Book Company Ltd.

ISBN 978-1-910184-80-6

Printed and bound in China.
Printed on paper from
sustainable sorces.

135798642

CONTENTS

Introduction	5
The Roman World	6
City and People	8
The Ruling Class	10
Ordinary Citizens	12
City Life	14
Bread and Circuses	16
Vespasian's Plans	18
Preparing the Site	20
Roman Builders	22
Layout and Materials	24
Decorations	26
Seats and Tickets	28
Behind the Scenes	30
Wild Beasts	32
Gladiators	34
Feasts and Fears	36
The Big Fight	38
Martyrs and Slaves	40
Later Centuries	42
Timespan	44
Glossary	47
Index	48

PAPER FROM
SUSTAINABLE
FORESTS

THE ROMAN COLOSSEUM

Written by
Fiona Macdonald

Series created by
David Salariya

Illustrated by
Mark Bergin

SCRIBO

It took many months of careful planning to design a structure as big and as magnificent as the Colosseum. There was no large machinery to help build it. Parts of the Colosseum remain standing today.

Introduction

THE ENORMOUS OVAL-SHAPED amphitheater known as the Colosseum has stood close to the middle of Rome for 1,900 years. Ever since it was first completed, in 96 CE, people have admired its vast size and bold design. It measures 187 feet (57 meters) high, 617 feet (188 meters) across (at its widest point) and 1,729 feet (527 meters)—about a third of a mile—around the outside. Many legends have grown up about it, the most famous being that if the Colosseum is ever destroyed, then the city of Rome will also be destroyed.

Throughout the ages, the Colosseum has been admired as a magnificent building, and an impressive feat of engineering. But today most people would find little to admire in the "entertainments" that were staged in it: the thousands of gladiators, captives, and criminals who died fighting in the Colosseum, or the millions of animals that were slaughtered in the Colosseum's wild-beast shows to satisfy the spectators' lust for blood. They also remember the hundreds of brave Christian men and women who were killed because of their beliefs.

But to the ancient Romans, the Colosseum was a noble monument to a powerful ruling family, a popular place of entertainment, and a sacred arena where "holy and ancient games" (as one Roman writer described them) were staged.

THE ROMAN WORLD

THE COLOSSEUM was built during the first century CE, when the Roman empire was growing ever richer and more powerful. Roman governors, backed up by Roman armies, ruled over conquered territories, and administered Roman laws. Roman tax collectors sent money levied from conquered peoples back to the emperors' treasury in Rome. Roman merchants went all over the empire, buying valuable goods to sell to rich citizens in Rome.

Corn, wine, honey, olive oil, and spices came from the empire's farms. Valuable raw materials, such as marble, metal, and wool, and luxury goods like silk, papyrus, glass, furs, and jewels were seized by soldiers, paid as tribute, or purchased by wealthy citizens.

The Roman empire at its largest and most powerful, around 100 CE. The empire stretched from Scotland to the Middle East.

SCANDINAVIA

Slavs

North Sea

Saxons

Britons   London   BRITAIN

GERMANY

ITALY

FRANCE

Marseille

Rome   Naples

SICILY

SPAIN

Carthage

Cordoba

NORTH AFRICA

The eagle was the symbol of the Roman empire.

In Roman times, the countries of present-day Europe did not exist. Instead, the land was occupied by many warring tribes. By 100 CE, the Romans had conquered most of these tribes. Only the northern Germans, the Scandinavians and the Slavs remained free.

The Roman empire reached its greatest size during the reign of Emperor Trajan (98–117 CE). But it stayed at this peak of power and prosperity for less than 100 years. By around 200 CE, its authority was declining and conquered people were preparing to rebel. The empire finally collapsed in 476. But the Colosseum, like many other magnificent Roman buildings, remained standing for future generations to see.

The greatest threat to the might of the Roman empire came from wild tribes, like the Huns and Goths, who lived on its north-eastern frontiers.

ASIA

Caspian Sea

Black Sea

GREECE

Athens

Corinth

MIDDLE EAST

Mediterranean Sea

EGYPT

Alexandria

CITY AND PEOPLE

"ROME, GODDESS of people and continents, nothing can equal you, and nowhere can approach your power." That was what the Roman poet Martial wrote around 80 CE. The heart of the Roman empire, Rome spread over the famous "Seven Hills", the legendary home of the city's first inhabitants. People arriving in Rome from distant lands were astonished by the riches and beauty of the central districts of the city. They gazed in wonder at the majestic temples and the fine statues of heroes, goddesses, and gods. They admired the extravagantly decorated palaces and beautiful gardens belonging to wealthy noble families and the dignified, spacious public buildings built by earlier rulers of Rome.

They strolled, dazzled, through the great Forum—a market-place where merchants sold goods from all over the known world. They stared with respect at a noble senator, carried shoulder-high by slaves in a curtained litter, on his way to a meeting to decide the fate of nations. They joined the noisy, excited crowds watching—and betting on—chariot races at the Circus Maximus. Tired and dirty, they looked longingly at the cheap and relaxing public baths.

Important buildings in Rome:

1. Theatre of Marcellus 13 CE.

2. Temple of Emperor Trajan 98–117 CE.

3. Trajan's Forum (a huge shopping mall with office blocks above) 113 CE.

4. Temple of Jupiter Capitolinus (the city of Rome's own god) c.500 BCE and restored many times.

5. Temple of Mars (the god of war) 2 BCE.

6. Basilica (building for public meetings and administration) begun by Julius Caesar 49–44 BCE, completed by Augustus 30 BCE–14 CE.

7. Basilica built by Emperor Maxentius 307–313 CE.

8. Temple of Venus (goddess of love) and Roma (goddess of the city of Rome) c.10 BCE.

9. Temple of Jupiter (the Romans' most powerful god) 30 BCE–14 CE.

10. The Colosseum 72–96 CE.

11. Circus Maximus (huge race-track for chariot races) begun 329 BCE, rebuilt many times.

12. Aqueduct built by Emperor Nero 54–68 CE.

13. Temple of Claudius 41–54 CE.

City boundary

The city of Rome was surrounded by walls, strongly rebuilt during the reign of Emperor Aurelian (270–275 CE). Inside the walls were splendid public buildings, fine houses, statues, and other monuments. Outside the walls were the suburbs where ordinary people lived.

The Ruling Class

FOR NEARLY FIVE centuries (509 to 27 BCE), Rome was a republic. Elected officials ruled on behalf of the Roman people. In 27 BCE, after years of civil war, the old republic was swept away and emperors began to rule. Officially the emperor's title was *princeps* (first citizen) but, by the time the Colosseum was being built, Emperor Domitian (ruled 81–96 CE) was demanding to be hailed as "Master and God".

Like other emperors, Domitian claimed to be more than just a man. Past emperors were worshipped in temples built in their honor after they were dead. Domitian's proud title reveals the emperors' tremendous powers. Massive building projects, like the Colosseum, reveal their vast wealth.

Emperors were expected to rule with the advice of the Senate: an assembly of nobles who had all held senior government posts. The Senate could discuss government policies and pass resolutions (called *senatus consulta*) which had the force of law.

A member of the elite Praetorian Guard (top left), one of the most prestigious regiments within the Roman army. During the 2nd century CE, the Praetorian Guard played an important role in government. The members chose, and assassinated, several emperors.

A patrician (nobleman) making a speech in the Senate (assembly). Under the Republican system, the Senate was the chief governing body of Rome. Its members discussed (and often shaped) government policy and proposed new laws. Senators all came from patrician (noble) families; they had all held senior government posts. After the republic ended in 27 BCE, the number of senators was reduced, but the Senate still debated the emperor's actions and offered advice.

Although the rich and noble enjoyed many privileges, plenty of ordinary Roman citizens did too. Citizens could vote and they enjoyed civil rights that the poor, foreigners, and slaves did not.

A patrician family (left). Patricians were rich and influential. Their wealth came from inherited property. Most patricians owned vast estates in the country which were worked by slaves.

Many patrician families also owned splendid houses and gardens in the city of Rome, with large rooms full of fine furniture.

Many emperors chose to ignore the Senate and follow the advice of palace servants, family, and friends. If this advice was good, and the emperor was wise, then Rome and its empire might be well governed. But if the advice was bad, then problems lay ahead.

ORDINARY CITIZENS

WE DO NOT KNOW the exact population of Rome during the time the Colosseum was being built (72–96 CE), but historians estimate that it was around one million in 100 CE. A few Roman families were nobles, as rich, and sophisticated as the city itself. Many more were ordinary, hard-working tradesmen, and women, busy in occupations ranging from pastry-makers and perfumers to corn-merchants, silk-weavers, and cooks. Other poorer citizens survived on part-time work and state charity. But they were all proud to belong to the city of Rome.

Many of Rome's inhabitants were not "proper" citizens. Roman law allowed peoples from all over the empire to come to Rome, though they did not have full citizen's rights. There was also an enormous population of male and female slaves—around 400,000 in 100 CE.

Foreigners and (especially) slaves were governed by harsh laws. For example, a master or mistress could put their slave to death. But, increasingly, these laws came to matter less and differences in work and wealth between citizens came to matter more. Many foreigners and slaves found good jobs and prospered, while Roman-born citizens remained poor.

Right: A big block of apartments, called an *insula* (island), built in the 1st century CE to provide homes for the rapidly increasing population of Rome. City land was becoming expensive, so Roman engineers designed buildings several storys high to make maximum use of space. Water came from the public fountain and there might be a toilet in the courtyard.

Extra rooms on roof

Blocks of apartments had shops and offices at street level and cramped, drafty attic rooms under the roof. The biggest and best rooms were on the first floor.

A busy Roman street in a district where ordinary people lived. In the summer people liked to spend time out of doors, away from their small, cramped homes. Many streets were lined with shops and stalls. There were taverns selling hot food and wine, and public bathrooms and water-fountains on many street corners.

Apartment roof used for storage

Litter

Shops

Street

City Life

AROUND 117 CE, the Roman poet Juvenal wrote, "How much happier is it to be a rich man's slave than a free-born citizen." Though they remained proud of their free-born Roman status, the ordinary citizens of Rome had been feeling dissatisfied for years.

One major complaint was about living conditions. Away from the grand central part of the city the streets of Rome were noisy, smelly, and dirty. Houses and apartments were ramshackle and crowded. People lived in fear of muggers, burglars, and fires.

Another complaint concerned the enormous wealth and power of the few rich families and their slaves. Many slaves were well trained: they worked as doctors, scribes, and accountants. Roman law allowed masters and mistresses to free their slaves (who could then earn high salaries), or leave them large sums of money in their wills. Successful, wealthy slaves and ex-slaves were resented by many ordinary Romans.

But the most serious complaint was the food. So many people lived in the city that wages were low and food prices high. Supplies were unpredictable, too. Around half the people (about 150,000 families in 100 CE) could not earn enough money to buy food for their families. They relied on free grain from the government to avoid starvation.

When harvests failed and grain supplies ran short, as they did in 6 CE, the citizens who relied on free food from the state rioted outside government buildings.

Wheat and barley to make bread to feed Rome's citizens were carried by ship from the fertile farmlands of Egypt, the vast plains of eastern Europe, and the shores of the Black Sea—all part of the Roman empire. Olive oil, wine, and fruit were also imported. All these foods were brought to Ostia, Rome's port, about 12 miles (20 kilometers) from the city.

Emperor Nero (ruled 54–68 CE) ordered a new aqueduct to bring fresh drinking water to the people of Rome.

Lead pipe for water *Street level*

Subsoil

In Ostia (left), streets where wealthy merchants and ship-owners lived were built with well-planned drains and sewers.

Brick-lined drains

Roman cargo ships (below) were heavy and bulky. They were powered by sails and oars, but few went far in winter because of storms.

Bread and Circuses

Statue of Jupiter *Plunder*

A triumphal procession. Victorious Roman generals were honored with a triumphal

procession through the streets of Rome. Military standard-bearers led the way.

Then came statues of the gods. Jupiter, the Romans' principal god, came first.

After the gods came slaves carrying heaps of rich plunder from conquered lands.

EMPERORS AND SENATORS knew that if the Roman people went hungry they would riot. Angry mobs would rampage through the streets, looting, and killing. To prevent this, the government provided free entertainments as well as free food.

Together, these "gifts" were known as "bread and circuses"—a "circus" was an arena where chariot races were held—and they cost a vast amount. Money for food came from taxes, but entertainments were paid for by emperors or nobles from their own wealth.

There was an historic reason for this. In ancient Roman times, sports festivals had originally been staged in honor of the gods. Taking part in them, or even just watching, had been a religious act. Building a huge sports arena, like the Colosseum, had religious significance, too.

Human and animal sacrifices had also been part of ancient Roman religion. So staging fights between gladiators, or between men, and animals, was a way of making a religious offering.

Above: Masks worn by actors in tragic (left) and comic (right) plays.

Roman playwrights wrote about famous gods and heroes, myths, and legends, and everyday life. The bronze statue (right) shows a popular character in Roman plays—a cheeky slave.

Men, women, and children all acted on the Roman stage. The Emperor Nero believed he had acting talent and liked taking part in plays.

The second half of the procession contained captured enemy chiefs, more prisoners, and their weapons.

Captive chieftains

Lictors (government officials) carried "fasces", bundles of axes and sticks, as a sign of state power.

Lictors

Musicians

Bulls for sacrifice

Prisoners

Musicians followed, and behind them came priests leading animals for sacrifice to the gods.

With this group were men armed with axes for killing the sacrificial animals.

Enemy prisoners bound in chains came next. They, too, were often killed.

Behind the prisoners marched soldiers blowing wild-sounding war-trumpets.

Clay or bone tokens (far left) were used like tickets. Small clay figures (left) were made of the most popular actors.

Chariot racing and races by jockeys on horseback were very popular, and very dangerous, Roman spectator sports.

Rich Romans paid for sports and fights to mark important occasions in their lives, such as getting a top government job. They knew that entertainment was politically useful and hoped it would also please the gods.

Senators and judges followed the general.

The victorious troops marched at the rear.

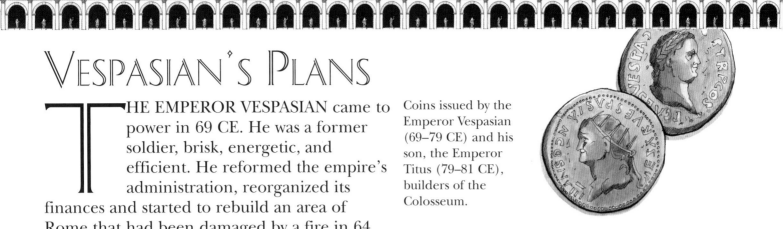

VESPASIAN'S PLANS

THE EMPEROR VESPASIAN came to power in 69 CE. He was a former soldier, brisk, energetic, and efficient. He reformed the empire's administration, reorganized its finances and started to rebuild an area of Rome that had been damaged by a fire in 64 CE. As part of his rebuilding scheme, he planned a huge public arena to be named after his family, the Flavians.

Vespasian's "Flavian" arena (which we now call the Colosseum) was designed as a typical Roman amphitheater: a circular (or oval) arena with a central stage surrounded by rows of seats. It was similar to, but much larger than, the Theatre of Marcellus, which had opened in Rome in 13 CE.

Coins issued by the Emperor Vespasian (69–79 CE) and his son, the Emperor Titus (79–81 CE), builders of the Colosseum.

Carving from the Roman city of Trier (in present-day Germany) showing a tax collector seated at his counting-table, while a slave carries away a sack of money paid by conquered German tribes. Taxes like this helped pay for the Colosseum.

Captured enemy soldiers were forced to fight to the death in public open spaces to entertain crowds. The captives were surrounded by a circle of well-armed soldiers to stop them running away.

The earliest Roman theaters had segment-shaped tiers of seats (left) made of strong wooden beams.

Theatre at Epidaurus, Greece, built in the 3rd century BCE. Roman architects often copied Greek designs.

Amphitheaters developed from earlier Greek and Roman theaters built for performances of music and plays. Their design was also influenced by small, temporary arenas made out of wooden fences, where fights, and plays were staged in the open air.

Roman engineers realized that a circular amphitheater could seat an audience twice the size of earlier, semicircular theaters and still give spectators a good view.

Right: Circular Roman amphitheater built at Nîmes, in southern France, 1st century CE.

Circular amphitheatres were used for all kinds of entertainment. Sometimes the floor was waterproofed with wood and canvas and flooded. Then mock sea-battles (left) were staged.

Many buildings in central Rome were destroyed by fire in 64 CE. Vespasian took the motto "*Roma Resurgens*" (Rome arising from the ashes) as the theme for his reign.

Preparing the Site

THE COLOSSEUM covered an area of about 53,820 square feet (5,000 square meters). It was surrounded by a wide sidewalk and cobbled streets. Roman engineers planned the building and its surroundings so that 50,000 spectators could come and go easily without getting crushed, panicking, or causing a riot.

Their clever planning meant that an enormous area had to be cleared before building work could start. This was not an easy task. The site was next to the ruins of the Golden House, a splendid palace which had been built for Emperor Nero (54–68 CE), and which contained the marshy remains of a large lake, part of the beautiful gardens that had surrounded Nero's home. This had to be drained and stabilized with layers of hard-packed gravel and soil.

The Colosseum's builders left in place a massive statue, almost 130 feet (40 meters) high, of Nero. They would have been very surprised to learn that this statue would give their building a new name.

Emperor Vespasian was a good businessman too, carefully checking the plans and budgets for the Colosseum.

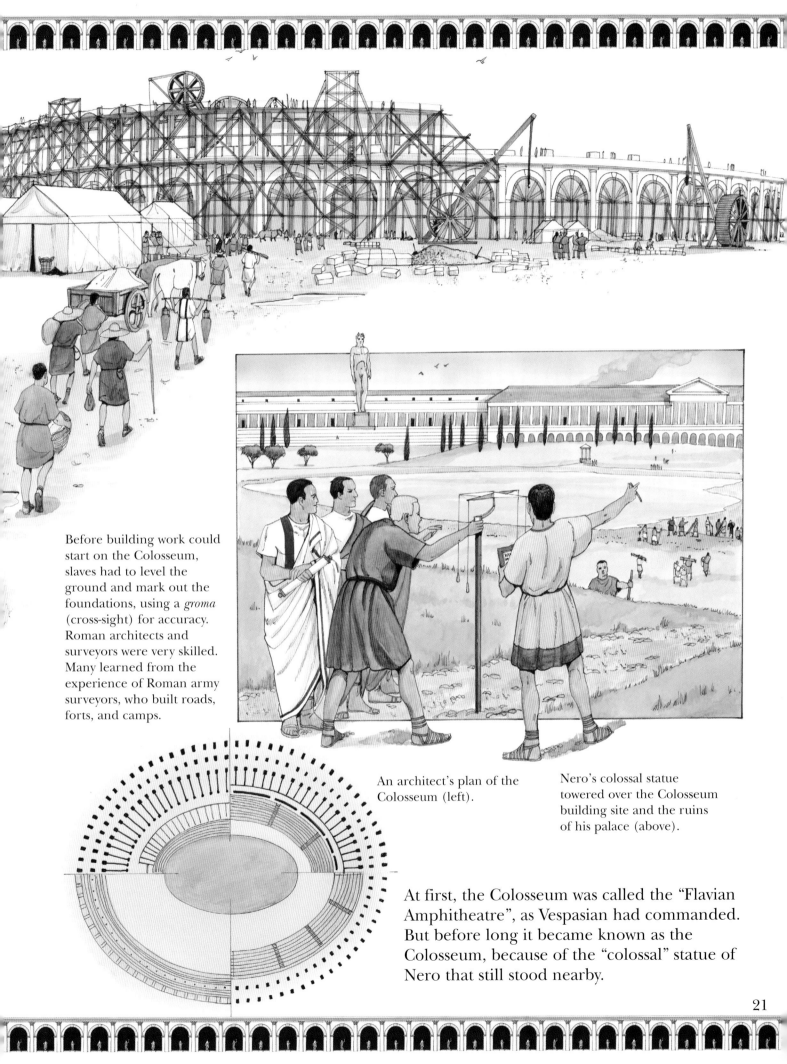

Before building work could start on the Colosseum, slaves had to level the ground and mark out the foundations, using a *groma* (cross-sight) for accuracy. Roman architects and surveyors were very skilled. Many learned from the experience of Roman army surveyors, who built roads, forts, and camps.

An architect's plan of the Colosseum (left).

Nero's colossal statue towered over the Colosseum building site and the ruins of his palace (above).

At first, the Colosseum was called the "Flavian Amphitheatre", as Vespasian had commanded. But before long it became known as the Colosseum, because of the "colossal" statue of Nero that still stood nearby.

Roman Builders

ROMAN WORKERS organized themselves into corporations or guilds, which tried to regulate wages and hours of work. They also maintained quality standards and gave emergency help to members in need.

There were guilds for the highly trained draftsmen and surveyors, as well as for skilled building workers: masons, carpenters, ironworkers, and demolition experts. There were also many ordinary laborers, transport workers, and slaves.

Work started at the site in 72 CE. The builders made such good progress that the arena was ready to be dedicated in 80 CE, although work on the seating and decoration continued for another sixteen years.

Even with gangs of slaves to help the master craftsmen, building the Colosseum was a mammoth undertaking. Roman builders had no big machines, apart from hoists, to help them; all construction relied on muscle power.

Roman quarry workers cut huge blocks from the rock-face using simple technology. First they drilled grooves in the rock.

Then they hammered wooden wedges into the grooves and poured water on them. The wet wood swelled, splitting the rock into blocks.

Finally the blocks were trimmed to exact size and shape using sharp metal chisels and wooden mallets.

Roman roads were expertly made. First, a wide trench was dug. Then it was filled with layers of sand, rough stone blocks, and pebbles mixed with gravel. It was finished with a layer of paving stones.

Builders' tools:
1 & 5. Pincers.
2 & 6. Squares (for measuring right angles.)
3 & 7. Chisels.
4. Plumb-level (to check walls were straight).
8. Ax.
9. Metal cutters.
10. Stone drill.

Stone was quarried about 18 miles (30 kilometers) away, then carried to Rome in ox-wagons along a specially built road. Bricks had to be fired and brought to the site, stone blocks had to be cut and carved to shape, massive wooden scaffolding had to be constructed and thousands of tons of concrete had to be mixed.

A day in the life of a builder:
6 am (dawn) Gets up, puts on tunic, and sandals.

6.30 am Has a simple breakfast of bread and water with his family.

7 am Arrives at building site. Gets instructions for work from foreman.

10 am Busy helping to make a solid wooden scaffolding to support the next stone arch.

11. 30 am Lunch with workmates: bread, cheese, fruit and water to drink.

12 noon Back to work, helping to haul blocks of stone to build the archway.

2 pm Work is over for the day, so goes to the public baths with some friends.

5 pm Buys ready-cooked food (meat pies and fig and honey cakes) to take home for dinner.

LAYOUT AND MATERIALS

THE LAYOUT of the Colosseum was simple: a high outer wall lined inside with sloping tiers of seats, with terraces, and walkways in between. Below the rows of seats was a promenade, where spectators might walk and talk with their friends during the lunchtime interval between shows.

The architects and engineers who planned the Colosseum's layout also had to choose the most suitable building materials. It would have been impractical to make the entire building out of solid stone because it would soon have collapsed under its own weight. So they used tiers of strong, but much lighter, stone arches for the outer walls. The rest of the building was constructed around a framework of tall stone columns that were filled in with cheaper, lighter materials.

Limestone blocks were used for this framework and to face the walls. They were carefully trimmed to shape, then fastened together with metal clamps. Several different types of material were used for "filling in". Tufa (a tough volcanic stone) was used for the lower walls, and concrete (a Roman invention) and brick were used for the upper walls. The ceiling-vaults were made of pumice, a soft volcanic stone.

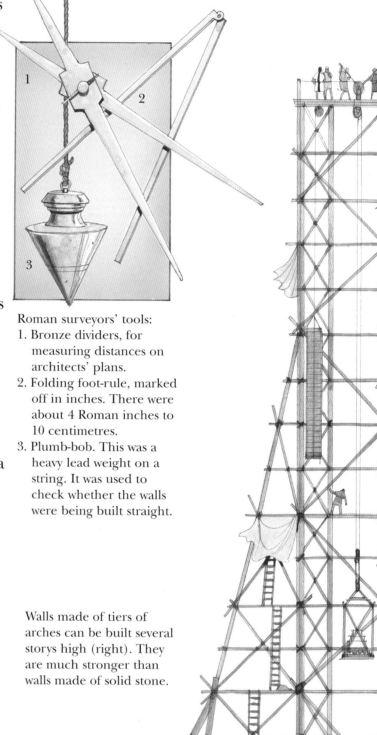

Roman surveyors' tools:
1. Bronze dividers, for measuring distances on architects' plans.
2. Folding foot-rule, marked off in inches. There were about 4 Roman inches to 10 centimetres.
3. Plumb-bob. This was a heavy lead weight on a string. It was used to check whether the walls were being built straight.

Keystone

Arches were built over a wooden framework called centring. It held the stone pillars at either side of the arch in place and stopped the wedge-shaped stones falling out while the arch was being built. Once the keystone, the stone in the center of the arch, was in place, all the stones locked together and the centring could be removed.

Walls made of tiers of arches can be built several storys high (right). They are much stronger than walls made of solid stone.

Stone was raised with large wooden hoists. These were powered by treadmills, huge wooden wheels turned by men walking up steps inside.

Treadmill

Hoist

Standing area for the poor, slaves, and

Women's seats behind wall

Walkway

Second tier of seats

First tier of seats

Arena

Promenade

DECORATIONS

THE EMPEROR VESPASIAN died in 79 CE. His sons Titus (reigned 79–81 CE) and Domitian (81–96 CE) became emperors after him. They, too, were successful soldiers, but not as good rulers as their father. Domitian was also an extremely cruel man.

The huge seating area inside the Colosseum was far too big to be covered by a wooden roof. So canvas awnings, called *velaria* (above), were made. They could be pulled across to shelter spectators from rain or sun. They were operated by former sailors, who were used to handling big sails on Roman cargo ships.

The walls of the Colosseum (left) were decorated with carved stone columns. As was the custom, these columns were arranged in a set order: heavy "Doric" columns on the ground, lighter "Ionic" columns on the first floor and elaborate "Corinthian" columns on the third floor. The top (fourth) floor columns were decorated with stone acanthus leaves.

Middle: Sailors and sailmakers working to install canvas awnings. Bottom: The Colosseum with the canvas awning pulled across to shelter the spectators.

The Colosseum was decorated with thousands of statues made of marble or metal. They stood under the arches on the first and second floors.

War shields adorned the Colosseum's outer walls.

Roman sculptors chose popular topics for their statues: gods and goddesses, famous athletes, heroes, and emperors.

1. Making a metal statue: The Romans used the "lost-wax" process to make metal statues. First, a full-size clay model was made (above).

2. The finished model was coated in wax, then covered in clay (right). Small pipes were stuck through the clay.

3. The clay-covered statue was heated. The wax ran out (above) and molten metal was poured in (left) to replace it.

Both Titus and Domitian continued their father's great building project. Like him, they wanted to keep the citizens calm and happy, to honor the gods (including, now, their dead father) and to bring glory to the Flavian family name.

They decided that one of the best ways of doing this was by decorating the Colosseum with a large number of statues and adorning the top of the outer wall with war shields. They hoped this would remind the people of their family's achievements in battle.

Roman sculptors were extremely skilled at producing lifelike portraits in metal, marble, and stone. The central sculpture was a splendid portrait statue of Vespasian himself, driving the four-horse chariot that was reserved for the emperor. It was placed, with an inscription recording his decision to build the Colosseum, over the entrance which only emperors and their guests could use.

4. When the metal had cooled and hardened, the clay covering was chipped off (right) and the statue was completed.

Seats and Tickets

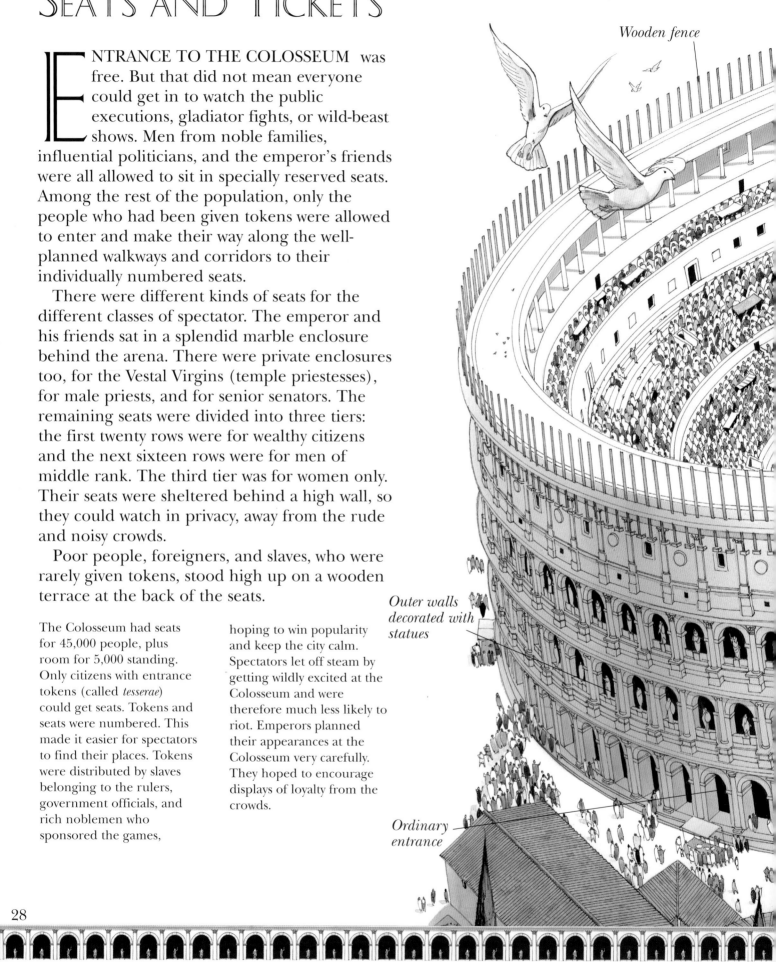

ENTRANCE TO THE COLOSSEUM was free. But that did not mean everyone could get in to watch the public executions, gladiator fights, or wild-beast shows. Men from noble families, influential politicians, and the emperor's friends were all allowed to sit in specially reserved seats. Among the rest of the population, only the people who had been given tokens were allowed to enter and make their way along the well-planned walkways and corridors to their individually numbered seats.

There were different kinds of seats for the different classes of spectator. The emperor and his friends sat in a splendid marble enclosure behind the arena. There were private enclosures too, for the Vestal Virgins (temple priestesses), for male priests, and for senior senators. The remaining seats were divided into three tiers: the first twenty rows were for wealthy citizens and the next sixteen rows were for men of middle rank. The third tier was for women only. Their seats were sheltered behind a high wall, so they could watch in privacy, away from the rude and noisy crowds.

Poor people, foreigners, and slaves, who were rarely given tokens, stood high up on a wooden terrace at the back of the seats.

The Colosseum had seats for 45,000 people, plus room for 5,000 standing. Only citizens with entrance tokens (called *tesserae*) could get seats. Tokens and seats were numbered. This made it easier for spectators to find their places. Tokens were distributed by slaves belonging to the rulers, government officials, and rich noblemen who sponsored the games, hoping to win popularity and keep the city calm. Spectators let off steam by getting wildly excited at the Colosseum and were therefore much less likely to riot. Emperors planned their appearances at the Colosseum very carefully. They hoped to encourage displays of loyalty from the crowds.

Wooden fence

Outer walls decorated with statues

Ordinary entrance

Arena

Outside sidewalk

The Colosseum had 80 different entrances: 76 were for the public, two were for the emperor and his friends, and two were used by gladiators. The gladiators marched into the arena through one of these entrances, and their dead bodies were dragged out through the other.

Emperor's entrance

MARK BERGIN MCMXCV

Behind the Scenes

The manager (left) and his staff looked after day-to-day building maintenance and repairs.

Workmen (below) built strong barricades around the arena and kept seats and walkways clean.

RUNNING A HUGE BUILDING like the Colosseum required a large staff and hard-working managers to organize them. Some Colosseum staff could be seen by the spectators as they swept and cleaned, guarded the entrances, and lugged heavy safety fences into place. But most people working at the Colosseum were less visible because they worked underground. While the gladiators fought and the lions roared overhead in the arena, dozens of workmen, and slaves were busy in the maze of corridors, lifts, stairs, and storerooms that lay hidden beneath the Colosseum, far away from public view.

Grooms (left) looked after the animals used for horse races, mock hunts, and wild-beast shows.

There were amphitheaters and gladiator fights in many Roman towns. In Pompeii, gladiators lived in the barracks (below). In Rome, gladiators lived in barracks (now destroyed) built by Emperor Claudius (41–54 CE).

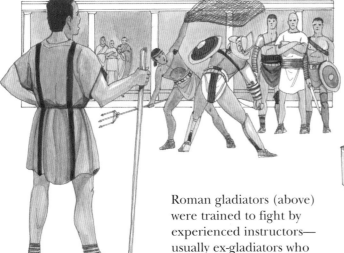

Roman gladiators (above) were trained to fight by experienced instructors— usually ex-gladiators who had survived many fights.

Some tasks were quite pleasant: making stage-sets, painting replica boats for mock sea-fights, or looking after the actors who staged early-morning comic shows. But most were not. Staff working underground had to guard frightened prisoners awaiting death, watch—and listen—as whole families of Christians were burnt alive, or torment wild animals in their cages until they were in a proper state of fury to "perform". At the end of the show, they had to dispose of the bodies and clear up the blood.

Many gladiator fights and wild-beast shows were staged against a background of painted scenery, like a stage set. This was made by skilled craftsmen and hauled into position with pulleys and ropes.

Notices advertising gladiator fights were put on walls and trees by slaves of the rich men paying for the shows.

Colosseum staff (below left) collected seat tokens from spectators as they arrived.

Slaves working for the Colosseum management had to remove the dead bodies.

Specialist engineers had to flood the arena when emperors wanted to stage mock sea-battles.

WILD BEASTS

Mosaic showing captive wild animals being taken to Rome.

Many wild animals, like this antelope (right), suffered on the way to Rome.

There was an enormous demand for animals to be used in Colosseum shows. All over the Roman empire huntsmen and soldiers hunted and captured all the wild beasts they could find.

HUNTING WAS ONE of the Romans' most popular sports. But, of course, this was not possible in the city of Rome. So wild-beast shows were staged in amphitheaters like the Colosseum, where trapped animals, brought from hundreds of miles away, were let loose to be chased by gladiators or to fight captive criminals. Sometimes, the sheer scale of death was horrifying. When Emperor Titus opened the Colosseum in 80 CE, over five thousand animals were killed on the first day of the games. Today, many people respect the natural environment and try to protect the creatures in it. But the Romans, like many other people in the past, had different views.

Stone carving (left) of gladiators fighting lions and bears.

Mosaic of a gladiator fighting against a wolf.

To the Romans, nature was savage and had to be tamed. Wild beasts lacked the qualities of humans, so, the Romans thought, it was fine to kill them for fun.

This attitude had terrible consequences. During the centuries when wild-beast shows were common (from 105 BCE until 532 CE), several species became extinct in Roman lands. Hippopotami died out in Egypt, lions in the Middle East, and elephants in North Africa. Today many people would say that watching such mindless killing harmed the spectators, too.

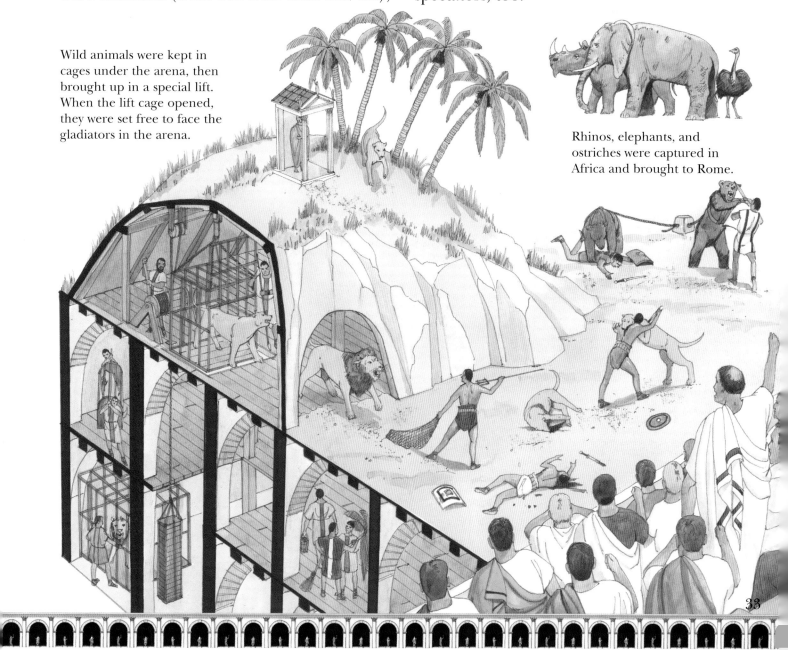

Wild animals were kept in cages under the arena, then brought up in a special lift. When the lift cage opened, they were set free to face the gladiators in the arena.

Rhinos, elephants, and ostriches were captured in Africa and brought to Rome.

Thracian gladiator (right) armed with a short sword and small shield. The other gladiator (far right) is called a *retiarius* and is armed only with a trident and a net.

Magnificent helmet, decorated with little statues, and feathers, worn by a successful gladiator, plus his short sword, or *gladius*.

Charioteer (right) wearing a helmet, tunic, and riding boots. He carries a horse-whip. A fully armed gladiator (far right) was known as a *Samnite*, after a war-like tribe that once lived near Rome, or a *secutor* (cutter), because he cut off men's lives.

GLADIATORS

GLADIATORS WERE the superstars of Roman public games. Although a few achieved fame and riches, on average, half the gladiators involved in any particular fight were likely to be killed.

Who became gladiators? Some men had no choice. Trainers bought them at the slave-market because they looked strong and fit for fighting. The trainers took them home to rented barracks, fed them, housed them, and trained them in combat skills. But they never let them go. These slave-gladiators were kept locked up like prisoners and had to fight at their trainer's command. Trainers hired out teams of gladiators to rich men wanting to put on a show. They made a lot of money.

Gladiators marched into the arena wearing cloaks of purple—the emperor's color. They were accompanied by musicians blowing war-trumpets.

They circled the arena, then stopped before the emperor's box, and bowed to him, saying, "Hail, Emperor. We who are about to die salute you."

Each Colosseum show usually started in the morning with cruel comic duels fought by women or people with physical disabilities.

Defeated gladiators (left) raised a finger of the left hand, to show they were begging the emperor for mercy. If he gave the thumbs-up signal, they lived.

Gladiators were often mismatched. Romans enjoyed seeing men fight desperately.

If the emperor turned his thumb downwards, they were killed by a slave dressed as Pluto, the god of the underworld (above). He hit them on the forehead with a hammer.

Some poor young men joined a trainer's team because it seemed the only alternative to starvation. They thought it worth risking their lives for a few months of good food, plus a faint chance of glory. Other volunteers included rich, daredevil young men, addicted to thrills and violence. Perhaps they were rather like racing-drivers today, though the risks they faced were far greater.

A few women, seeking dangerous excitements, tried to train as gladiators, too. But they were banned from the Colosseum and all other sports arenas in 200 CE.

Victorious gladiators (above) were given rich prizes and allowed to hang their weapons in the Temple of Hercules.

Top gladiators (left) attracted many fans, especially rich women.

FEASTS AND FEARS

THE COLOSSEUM has been called "a torture-chamber and a human-slaughterhouse". No wonder many gladiators facing a fight and captives and convicts awaiting execution spent their last night in misery and despair. Only the Christians faced death joyfully, sure of a new and better life in heaven.

On the evening before a fight the emperor or noble paying for the games would arrange a lavish feast and invite all the gladiators to share the meal together. Some gladiators ate little, so they would be alert for the fight next day. Others ate greedily, knowing it might be their last meal.

Roman mosaic showing ingredients for a rich seafood meal (right). Gladiators feasted on luxury foods at public banquets the night before a big fight in the Colosseum.

Successful gladiators often became very rich. But they knew they would not live long. They dictated their wills to professional scribes (above).

The Roman men and women who dined with gladiators before a fight enjoyed the knowledge that many of their fellow diners might be dead the next day.

Roman scribes wrote with quill pens on parchment or used wax-tablets and styluses like these.

Music was a more pleasant and peaceful form of entertainment. Popular Roman instruments included:
1. Sistrum.
2. Pipe.
3. Double flute.
4. Cymbals.
5. Trumpet.
6. Panpipes.

Many Roman games were much less bloodthirsty than gladiator fights. Gambling with dice and throwing knucklebones were both very popular.

Carved ivory game counter (top) showing girl with double flute.

Mosaic (above) showing double-flute player and dancing girl.

Members of the public were invited to watch this unpleasant feast and, occasionally, to join in. The brave, brutal gladiators fascinated many Roman citizens, including noblewomen and emperors' wives. They watched all their heroes' battles, cheering them as they entered the Colosseum on the day of the fight. Emperor Commodus (180–192 CE) was said to be the son of a famous gladiator, with whom his mother had had a secret love affair. Certainly, Commodus enjoyed fighting at the Colosseum. He was assassinated there, while dressed in gladiator's clothes.

Before a fight, gladiators were driven to the Colosseum in carts. Then they formed themselves into a procession to make a dramatic entrance. Well-wishers dropped gifts of flowers to their favorite gladiators as they entered the Colosseum.

THE BIG FIGHT

A PARTICULARLY LARGE FIGHT between gladiators was called a *hoplomachia*. After the gladiators had paraded around the arena, their weapons were checked, and the battle-order was announced. Duels might be arranged according to a master-plan for the day's entertainments, or chosen simply by lot. The Colosseum orchestra—flutes, trumpets, horns, and an organ—played a fanfare and the fighting began. The gladiators slashed and stabbed savagely —a hesitant fighter would not last long. Trainers stood beside the arena, urging their best gladiators on to fresh victories.

Gladiators who managed to survive several fights might be offered the *rudis* by the emperor. This was a wooden sword and it meant that the gladiator could stop fighting. He could sell the silver trophies and gold medals he had won as prizes and retire.

Astonishingly, some of the most successful gladiators who had been offered the rudis gave it back, negotiated new contracts with their trainers and continued fighting. Perhaps they felt life was not worth living without the excitement, the shining armor, the thrill of battle, the smell of blood in the arena, and the roar of the bloodthirsty crowd.

Right: On the far side of the arena, a musician sounds a fanfare as the judge of the gladiators' fights proclaims a winner.

Below: Armor worn by gladiators:
1. Helmet to protect the face of a gladiator against one armed with a trident.
2. Metal shin protector fastened around the leg with leather straps.
3. Protective metal plate worn on a gladiator's left shoulder.
4. Metal guard worn on the right wrist.
5. Elaborately decorated metal shin guard. Armor like this was extremely expensive and was usually part of the prize given to victorious gladiators.
6. Bronze helmet worn by a *hoplomachus*, a very heavily armed gladiator.

Short sword

Joined metal armor
for sword arm

Heavy bronze helmet

If the emperor was not present at the Colosseum, the victorious gladiator decided whether his defeated opponent should live or die. He was urged on by the crowds. They cried "Habet!" ("He's had it!") or "Verbera!" ("Hit him!") or "Iugula! Iugula!" ("Kill! Kill!").

Chain-mail over shoulder

Secutor

Ornamented belt

Short kilt

Shield

Trident

Leg protector

Net

Retarius

39

In 73 BCE, a captive called Spartacus led a gladiators' revolt. Armed only with knives, he and his friends fought their way out of the gladiators' school and took refuge in the mountains. Many runaway slaves joined them and they became a formidable army. It was two years before they were defeated.

Martyrs and Slaves

THOUSANDS OF convicted criminals were killed in the Colosseum. Roman emperors thought that Christians were criminals too, because they would not worship the Roman gods. So many Christians were executed as enemies of the state, in various appalling ways.

The first Christian to be martyred (killed because of his faith) in the Colosseum was Ignatius of Antioch, in around 110 CE. Later, when Christian rulers came to power in Rome, Ignatius was honored as a saint.

Like ordinary criminals, Christians were often killed by hungry leopards or lions. A cruel story told how this idea for execution originated: a wooden lift containing a criminal accidentally broke, dropping him among the beasts in the arena. The watching crowd thought this was such a good joke that "throwing people to the lions" became a popular part of the Colosseum shows.

One Christian martyr, St Telemachus, died bravely (around 404 CE) in a very different way. He was outraged at the sight of slaves and prisoners being forced to fight until they died. He leaped into the arena and tried to part the fighting men. He was put to death for disrupting the games, but, soon, other people began to share his horror at the brutality of the Colosseum shows.

Spartacus died in battle, but the Romans crucified 6,000 of his comrades beside the Appian Way.

The Appian Way was the main road out of Rome. It ran for 100 miles (160 kilometers) to the city of Capua. After Spartacus's revolt, there was a crucified man every 98 feet (30 meters) for the road's entire length.

Christians and criminals were tied to wooden frames, then wheeled into the arena to be mauled by lions (left). Spectators were protected by an iron fence built around the edge of the arena to stop lions escaping. The mosaic below shows a Christian being killed by a leopard.

LATER CENTURIES

THE LAST GLADIATOR FIGHT was held in the Colosseum in 404 CE. After that, fights were banned on the orders of Emperor Honorius (395–423 CE). He was a Christian, and believed that many old Roman customs were sinful, including human sacrifices, and the Colosseum's gladiatorial games. But the bloody wild-beast shows in front of a cheering audience continued for at least another hundred years.

Over the centuries, the Colosseum became neglected. It was damaged by earthquakes, the statues were stolen and tonnes of its stones, were taken for new buildings.

In 1855, British botanist Richard Deakin published a book entitled *Flora of the Colosseum.* In it, he listed 420 different varieties of plant he had found growing wild on the neglected site, including:
1. Christ's thorn.
2. Anemone.
3. Asphodel.

Visitors to the Colosseum c.1780

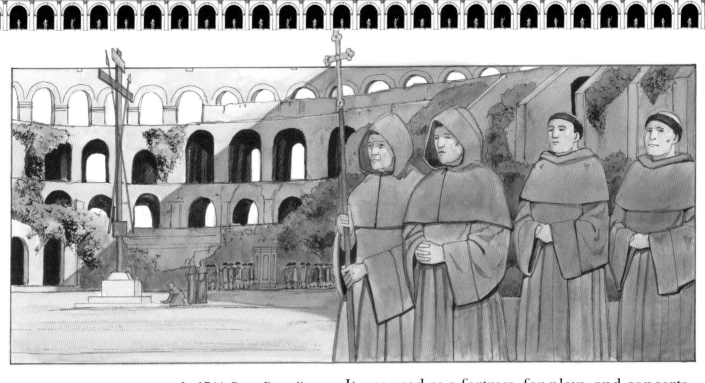

In the 18th and 19th centuries, wealthy young noblemen went on a "Grand Tour" of historic sites in Europe to complete their education. They were all very impressed by the Colosseum, even though it was half-ruined. One of the best descriptions of it was written in 1805 by the French Vicomte de Chateaubriand.

In 1744, Pope Benedict XIV gave orders for a huge wooden cross to be placed in the center of the Colosseum as a memorial to all the Christians who had been martyred there. He dedicated the whole building as a holy shrine and gave orders for a monk to preach a sermon in front of the memorial cross every Friday.

It was used as a fortress, for plays, and concerts (although the acoustics were terrible), for bullfights and even as stables for horses and cows. After 1650, it was visited by many wealthy tourists from many lands, eager to study Roman remains. Among them were the English poets Byron and Shelley, the German author Goethe and the French painter Corot.

The first serious attempts to preserve the Colosseum's structure were not made until the mid-19th century. Today, although the stonework has been carefully repaired, the Colosseum, like many ancient buildings, faces a new threat: air pollution.

TIMESPAN

All dates CE

72 Colosseum building work begins.

80 Emperor Titus leads dedication ceremony. First gladiatorial games at the Colosseum.

96 Colosseum completed.

c.110 St Ignatius of Antioch is the first-known Christian martyr to be killed in the Colosseum.

180–192 Emperor Commodus takes part in over 300 gladiatorial fights. He is assassinated at the Colosseum.

200 Women gladiators banned from Colosseum.

247–248 Emperor Philip the Arab stages a huge festival in the Colosseum to mark the thousandth anniversary of the founding of Rome.

253 Four Christian martyrs burned alive just outside the Colosseum.

320 The Colosseum is struck by lightning; remarkably unharmed.

399 Emperor Honorius bans gladiator training schools.

401 Captive Saxons, forced to fight as gladiators, strangle each other in the cells under the Colosseum rather than face a shameful death in front of Roman crowds.

c.404 Christian monk Telemachus leaps into the Colosseum arena to try to stop fights. He is executed.

404 Emperor Honorius abolishes pagan gladiatorial games.

410 Visigoth invaders attack Rome but do not damage Colosseum.

422 Earthquake damages Colosseum; repaired 467 and 472.

508 Further earthquake damage.

523 Last wild-beast show in Colosseum.

c.590 Colosseum arena overgrown by grass.

604 Grass growing on Colosseum walls.

735 The Venerable Bede, a Christian monk, is first to record the name "Colosseum" in writing.

800 Christian pilgrims start to travel to Rome; admire remains of Colosseum.

847 Further earthquake damage.

1084 Normans invade Rome; devastate area around the Colosseum.

1144 Colosseum turned into a fortress by noble family, the Frangipani. Houses, taverns, workshops built nearby.

1150 Colosseum (wrongly) described as "Temple of the Sun" in guidebook *The Marvels of Rome*, written by a Christian monk.

1231 More earthquake damage.

1320 Colosseum clearly shown in first-known medieval drawing of the city of Rome.

1322 Colosseum used to stage bullfights.

1337 Italian poet Petrarch visits Colosseum.

1349 Further earthquake damage.

1381 Italian religious guilds use Colosseum to stage mystery (religious-story) plays.

1400 Colosseum stone used for new buildings in Rome.

1431 Renaissance scholar Poggio Bracciolini laments that Colosseum "is already half destroyed".

1451 Over 2,000 cartloads of stone removed from Colosseum on orders of Pope Nicholas I for use in new buildings.

1490s Passion plays performed in Colosseum at Easter, re-enacting the death of Jesus Christ.

1535 Black-magic rituals in Colosseum at night.

c.1550 Renaissance artists visit Colosseum to study details of Roman design.

1675 Colosseum now a store for chemicals used to make gunpowder.

1703 Further earthquake damage.

1744 Pope Benedict XIV erects memorial cross to Christians martyred in Colosseum. Arranges for weekly sermon to be preached there.

1750s Colosseum now surrounded by wild grassland, called the "Cow Pasture". Used as stable for horses and cows.

c.1750 Many tourists visit Rome and admire Colosseum. Local people comment "If the Colosseum could be picked up, tourists would carry it away."

c.1750–c.1800 Poets, painters, philosophers, and historians from all over Europe visit the Colosseum.

1812 French military architects clear away plants growing on Colosseum walls.

1817 British poet Lord Byron writes about Colosseum: "Heroes have trod this spot, 'tis on their dust ye tread."

1825 Pope Leo XII builds buttresses to support Colosseum walls.

1844 English novelist Charles Dickens calls Colosseum "the ghost of old Rome—a wicked, wonderful old city".

1850s Pope Pius IX organizes repairs to Colosseum.

1855 Deakin's *Flora of the Colosseum* published.

1878 American novelist Henry James writes short story "Daisy Miller". Daisy, a young tourist, goes to view romantic Colosseum ruins by moonlight, catches fever from its "villainous miasma" and dies.

1890s Area around Colosseum cleared of other buildings.

1912 Irish playwright George Bernard Shaw writes play *Androcles and the Lion* about a Christian captive who helps a timid lion in the Colosseum. They become friends and escape to freedom.

1951 Grand concert held to celebrate the fiftieth anniversary of Italian composer Giuseppe Verdi's death, but not a musical success, since the Colosseum's acoustics are bad.

1996 One thousand, nine hundred years since Colosseum building completed.

2000 Colosseum's seven-year restoration project completed.

GLOSSARY

Amphitheater A circular or oval-shaped building, consisting of an open central arena, surrounded by rows of seats.

Aqueduct A raised channel built to carry fresh water.

Arena (1) The central open space of an amphitheater. (2) A building used for sports contests or army displays, usually roofless.

Barracks A large building where soldiers eat and sleep.

Circus A long arena with curved ends, where chariot races and horse races were held.

Emperor The ruler of an empire. Usually had tremendous personal power.

Forum A large market-place in the middle of Rome and other Roman towns. Important as a meeting place, as well as for trading.

Games A word used to describe a variety of sporting events, including gladiator fights. Games had originally been staged in honor of the gods.

Gladiators Professional fighters who took part in battles arranged for public entertainment in Rome. Many of those who survived became popular heroes and won rich prizes.

Guild An organization of workers which aimed to provide training, control quality, fix wages, and offer welfare help.

Imperial Belonging to an empire.

Insula The Roman word for a block of apartments.

Litter A form of transport: a lightweight portable bed carried shoulder-high by slaves.

Martyrs People who are killed because of their religious beliefs.

Papyrus Paper made from reeds that grew in the River Nile, in Egypt.

Patricians The noble families of Rome.

Princeps The Roman emperor's title. It means "first" (among citizens with equal rights).

Pumice A lightweight stone, formed from cooled volcanic lava.

Republic A system of government in which the leaders are elected by the people. Republics do not have ruling families which hand on power from parents to children.

Rudis A wooden sword offered to a victorious gladiator by the emperor as a sign that he was free to retire.

Senate An assembly of respected men who had held top government posts. They offered advice to government leaders and could suggest new laws.

Senator A member of the Senate.

Tufa A grey stone, formed from layers of compressed volcanic dust.

Velaria Canvas awnings providing a roof to shelter spectators in the Colosseum.

Vestal Virgins Priestesses from noble families who guarded the "sacred flame" in a temple in the middle of Rome.

INDEX
Page numbers in bold refer to illustrations.

A
actors **16**, **17**, 31
amphitheaters 5, 18, **19**, 31, 32, 46
animals 5, **17**, 30, 31, **32**, **33**, 40, 41
apartments 12, **13**, 14
aqueduct **15**, 46
arches **23**, 24, **24**
architects 19, 21, 24
armor **34**, 38
army 6, **10**, **16**, 17

B
"bread and circuses" 16
bricks 23, 24
building materials 22, 23, 24
building workers 22, **23**

C
chariot races 16, **17**
Christians 5, 31, 36, 40, **41**, 42, **43**
columns 24, **26**
concrete 23, 24
craftsmen 22

D
drains **15**

E
Egypt 14, 33
Emperors 10, 11, 16, 27, 28, 29, 30, 35, 36, 37, 38, 39, 40, 46
  Aurelian 9
  Claudius 31
  Commodus 37
  Domitian 10, 26, 27
  Honorius 42
  Nero 15, 16, 20, **21**

Titus **18**, 26, 27, 32
Trajan **7**
Vespasian 18, **18**, 19, **20**, 26, 27
engineers 12, 19, 20, 24, 30
executions 28, 40
extinction of animals 33

F
Flavian family 18, 21, 27
food 12, 13, **23**, **26**
  free 14, 16
  riots **14**
fountains 12

G
Germans 7, 18
gladiators 5, 16, 28, 29, 30, 31, 32, **33**, 34, **35**, 36, 37, 38, **39**, 40, 42, 46
gods and goddesses 8, 16, **16**, 17, 27, **35**, 40
Goths 7
groma **21**

H
houses and homes **11**, 12, **13**, 14, 16
Huns 7

J
Jupiter **16**
Juvenal, Roman poet 14

L
lictors **16**

M
Martial, Roman poet 8

meals **23**, 36, **36**, 37
Middle East 6, 33
music and musicians **17**, 18, **34**, **37**, 38, **39**

N
North Africa 33

O
Ostia 14, 15, **14–15**

P
patricians **10**, **11**, 47
plays 16, 18
pollution 43
Pompeii 31
Praetorian Guard **10**
prisoners **16**, **17**, **18**, 31, 34, 40
pumice 24, 47

R
religion 16
riots 14, 16, 20, 28
roads **22**, 23, **41**
Roman empire 6, **6**, 7, 11, 12, 18
Rome, city of 5, 8–9, **8–9**, 11, 12, 13, 14, 15, 16, 18, **19**, 31, 32, 33, 41
Rome, republic of 10, 47
rudis 38, 47

S
sacrifices 16, 17, 42, 47
scaffolding 23, **23**
Scandinavia 7
scenery 30
sea-battles **19**, **30**, 31
seats 18, 22, 24, 26, 28

Senate 10, **10**, 11, 47
senators 8, 10, 16, **17**, 28, 47
sewers **15**
ships **14**, **15**, 26
shops **12**
slaves 10, 12, 14, **16**, **18**, **21**, 22, 28, 30, **30**, 34, 40
Slavs 7, 47
soldiers **16**, **17**, **18**, 26
Spartacus 34, 35
statues 8, **9**, 20, 21, 27, **27**, 42
stone for building **22**, 23, 24, **25**, 42
surveyors **21**, 22

T
tax collectors 6, **18**
taxes 6, 14
temples 8, **8**, **9**, 10, 35, 42
theaters 18, **18**
tokens for seats **17**, 28, **30**
tools **23**, 24
tourists 43
trade 6, 14
tufa 24, 47

V
Vestal Virgins 28, 47
Visigoths 44

W
walls 24, **26**
water 12, 15
weapons **38**
wild-beast shows 5, 28, 30, **31**, 32, 33, 42
women gladiators 35

First published in MCMXCVI as *Inside Story – The Roman Colosseum* by MacDonald Young Books © The Salariya Book Co Ltd MCMXCVI